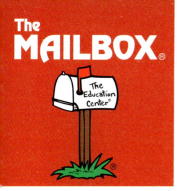

The MAILBOX®

Weste...

grades

Our best western activities and reproducibles from the 1999–2003 issues of *The Mailbox®* and *Teacher's Helper®* magazines

- **Literacy Ideas**

- **Math Activities**

- **Learning Centers**

- **Fine-Motor Activities**

- **Recipes**

- **Arts-and-Crafts Ideas**

Build Core Skills!

   And Much More!

Editorial Team: Becky S. Andrews, Kimberley Bruck, Diane Badden, Thad H. McLaurin, Sharon Murphy, Karen A. Brudnak, Juli Docimo Blair, Sarah Hamblet, Hope Rodgers, Dorothy C. McKinney

Production Team: Lori Z. Henry, Pam Crane, Rebecca Saunders, Jennifer Tipton Cappoen, Chris Curry, Sarah Foreman, Theresa Lewis Goode, Greg D. Rieves, Eliseo De Jesus Santos II, Barry Slate, Donna K. Teal, Zane Williard, Tazmen Carlisle, Kathy Coop, Marsha Heim, Lynette Dickerson, Mark Rainey, Karen Brewer Grossman

www.themailbox.com

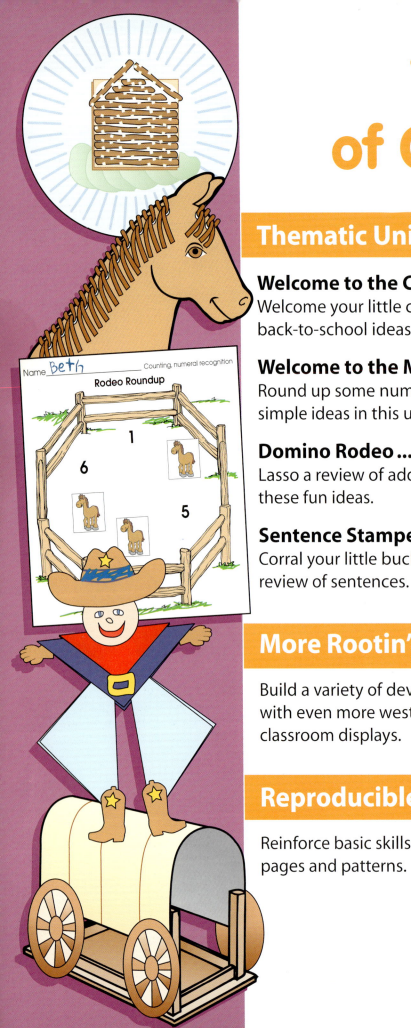

Table of Contents

Welcome to the Corral!

Get back in the saddle with these cowboy-themed, welcome-to-school ideas. Your youngsters will be off to a great start when you greet them with a big HOWDY!

ideas by Susan Bunyan and Susan DeRiso

Write 'em, Cowboy!

One week before school begins, rustle up some excitement about the **first day** by sending your youngsters a letter! To prepare, make a copy of the letter on page 8. Program the letter with your name, grade level, the school's name, the room number, and the day and time that school begins. Sign the letter, make a copy for each child, and then program each one with a different child's name. Next, make a yellow construction paper copy of the badge (page 9) for each child. Personalize each badge and then laminate it. Mail each child his letter and badge. On the first day of school, dress in your best cowpoke attire. Greet each youngster with a hearty "Howdy!" and then pin his badge to his clothing. (Be sure to have extra badges for unexpected arrivals.) Yee-ha! What a way to start the year!

Calling All Cows!

Caution! This cute cattle **display** may cause a stampede of admirers! To prepare this display, use an overhead or opaque projector to enlarge the cowboy (page 10) to make a bulletin board character. Attach the cowboy to a bulletin board. Next, use a length of twine or thin rope to create a lasso; then staple the lasso to the board and to the cowboy's hands. Title the board "Look Who's Rounded Up for Kindergarten!"

To prepare the cattle, enlarge the cow pattern on page 11 for each child. Cut out the cows and place them at a center along with a black washable ink pad. After each little cowpoke has moseyed on in, have her write her name on a cow. Have the child use the ink pad to make fingerprint spots on her cow. Then staple her completed cow inside the lasso on the bulletin board. Whoa, there! That's a mighty fine lookin' display!

Hats Off to You!

The result of this **name writing** activity is personalized cowboy hats! To make one hat, duplicate the large cowboy hat pattern (page 12) onto brown construction paper. Laminate the hat, and cut it out; then use a craft knife to create slits where indicated. Next, slide a 1½" x 24" strip of laminated paper through the slits as shown. Have each child use a permanent marker to write her name on the strip; then staple the strips to fit the child's head. Howdy, pardner!

Line Up!

Use this **numeral recognition** idea to line up your little cowpokes with ease! To prepare, use the pattern on page 13 to cut a pair of construction paper cowboy-boot shapes for each child in your class. Label each pair with a number. Laminate the boots; then tape the pairs in numerical order near your door. Direct your line leader to stand on the first pair of boots, the second child to stand on the second pair of boots, etc. When your little ones are lined up, have them recite the rhyme below; then giddy up and go!

When buckaroos line up with folks,
There are no pushes, shoves, or pokes.
Their hands are still and by their sides,
Feet ready for a quiet ride.
Giddy up!

Ready for a Rodeo

This lively **gross-motor** game will have your little ones kicking up their heels! To play, divide your youngsters into two relay teams; then line up each team facing a small chair. Give the second child in each line a small cowboy figure or a stuffed teddy bear. At the start signal, the first child in line gets on his hands and knees. The second child places the cowboy on the first child's back and says, "Giddy up!" The first child crawls to the chair and then back to the line while balancing the cowboy on his back. When he returns to the line, he tags the next team member and then places the cowboy on that child's back. The relay continues in this manner until each child has had a turn being a bronco. Yahoo!

A Place to Hang Your Hat

Center time will be organized and orderly with this idea. In advance, use the small hat pattern on page 9 to make a personalized, laminated cowboy hat for each child. Then punch a hole in the top of each hat. Next, make an enlarged copy of the cowboy (page 10) for each center in your classroom. Program each cowboy with the name of a different center. Then mount each cowboy near the appropriate center. Next, use a permanent marker to program each cowboy's hat with the number of children allowed at the center. Then attach the corresponding number of self-adhesive hooks near the cowboy. During center time, have each child choose a center with an available hook and then hang his hat on the hook. When he leaves the area, direct the child to take his hat with him, just like any good cowboy would do!

How the West Was Fun

Use this idea and transform your **reading area** into the Wild West. In advance, ask an appliance store for donations of several large boxes, such as refrigerator boxes. Remove the back panel from each box and set it aside. Use a craft knife to cut a door and windows; then paint the front of each box to resemble a western storefront. Next, cut a cactus shape from each of the back panels and then paint it green. When the paint is dry, use duct tape to attach each cactus to the end of a bookshelf. Or tape each cactus to a small chair and place it in the area. Add several beanbag chairs to the area, and stock the shelves with a collection of cowboy literature. It won't be hard to round up some readers with this idea!

Laura Taylor
Bellingham, WA

Getting in Shape

Reinforce **shape recognition** with this center idea. To prepare, use clear packing tape to tape lengths of rope or twine in different shapes on your floor. Next, cut out tagboard shapes that match the shapes of the ropes. For durability, laminate the tagboard shapes. Then place them in a cowboy hat. To use the center, a child pulls a shape from the cowboy hat and places it in the matching lasso.

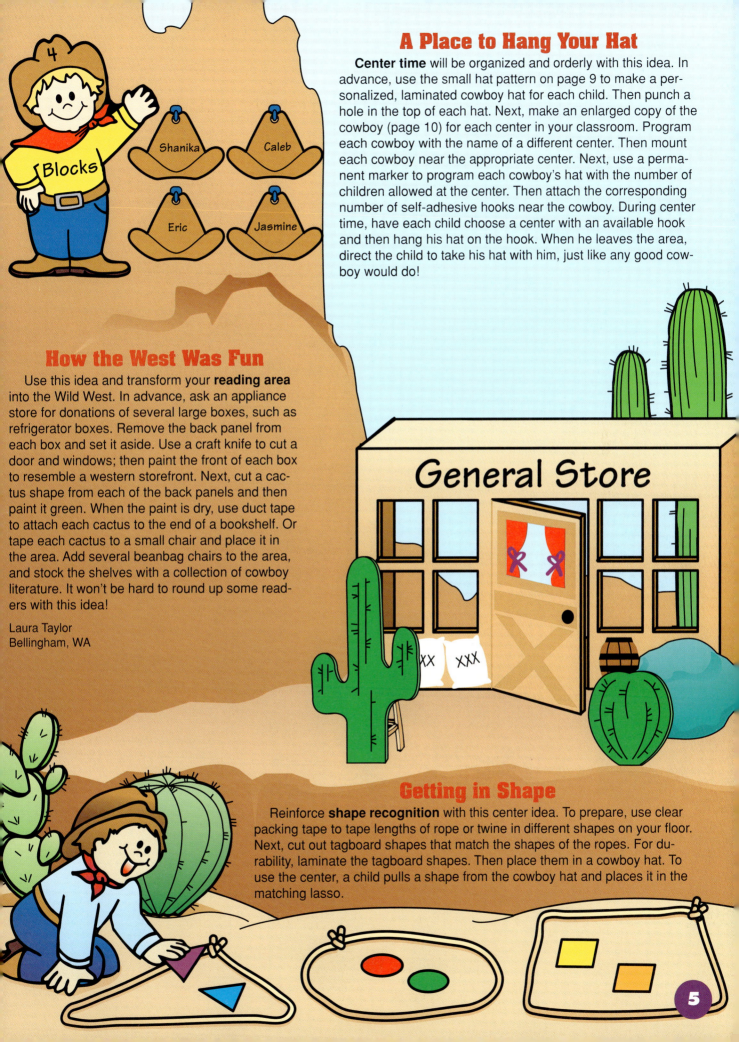

Blocks

Shanika   Caleb

Eric   Jasmine

General Store

My First Day
at the
Kindergarten
Corral!

Giddy-Up Getup

Make a happy **first-day memory** for each youngster by having an adult volunteer snap a photograph of the child in a cowhand getup. To prepare, stock your dress-up area with a variety of child-sized western wear such as bandanas, chaps, vests, and cowboy boots and hats (at your discretion). Invite each child to visit the area and don a western outfit. If you created western storefronts described in "How the West Was Fun" (page 5), have each child stand in front of a store, and then have your volunteer take her picture. (Develop a double set of prints. Set aside one set of prints to use in "A Rodeo Portfolio" below.) Mount each photograph on a sheet of construction paper and then add the title "My First Day at the [grade level] Corral!" Both parents and children will be thrilled with this cowhand keepsake.

A Rodeo Portfolio

Use this **class book** to help each child get acquainted with the other cowpokes in her class. Duplicate page 14 for each child; then have her write to complete each sentence. Next, glue the child's duplicate photo from "Giddy-Up Getup" onto the top half of the paper. Bind the completed pages between construction paper covers and then add a title. If desired, send the book home with a different student each night and encourage the child to introduce her classmates to her family. After each child has had a chance to share the book with her family, place it in your reading area for youngsters to enjoy.

Mrs. DeRiso's
Kindergarten
Cowhands

Cowpoke __Tina__

My favorite color is __blue__

I like to eat __fried chicken__

I am __5__ years old.

Rope 'em In!

Calling all cowboys and cowgirls! It's time to lasso! Your little cowpokes will have a rootin'-tootin' time with this outdoor activity that promotes **eye-hand coordination**. To prepare, make several large rings out of rope (or use several Hula-Hoop® toys). Place the ropes in an open area; then set a rocking horse some distance away from the ropes. (If a rocking horse is not available, use a small chair.) Invite each child to try to lasso the horse by tossing a rope ring over its head. Gotcha!

Jennifer Barton
Elizabeth Green School
Newington, CT

Tasty Tumbleweeds

Follow the recipe on the right to create a unique **snack** that will have little taste buds tumbling! To keep your little cowhands from getting parched, serve this snack with some genuine cow juice (milk).

Tasty Tumbleweeds

Ingredients for one snack:
1 tbsp. cream cheese
1 tbsp. honey
2 tbsp. powdered milk
2–3 tbsp. shredded wheat
small paper cup
craft stick
sheet of waxed paper

Wash hands. Use the craft stick to mix together the cream cheese and honey in a small paper cup. Add powdered milk little by little until the dough is no longer sticky. Turn the dough onto a sheet of waxed paper; then roll the dough into a ball. Sprinkle shredded wheat onto the waxed paper. Roll the dough in the wheat.

Michael had a rootin'-tootin' boot-scootin' day!

Give 'em the Boot!

Present each of your young cowpokes with this **end-of-the-day treat**, and watch him ride off into the sunset with a smile! Make one copy of the boot pattern on page 13. Program the boot as shown. Then make a construction paper copy of the programmed boot for each child. Have each youngster write his name at the top of his boot and then cut it out. Then cut two slits in each boot and slip a lollipop through it as shown.

WANTED!

_____
(Student's name)

Howdy, pardner!

My name is _____
(Teacher's name)

and I need YOU to come down and help me out at the

_____ **Corral! Please meet me at**
(Grade level)

_____
(School)

in _____ **on** _____ **at** _____ **:** _____
(Room)   (First day of school)   (Time)

Bring along the enclosed ranger badge, so I'll know

you're not horsin' around!

Happy Trails!

_____
(Teacher's signature)

Note to the teacher: Use the letter with "Write 'em, Cowboy!" on page 3.

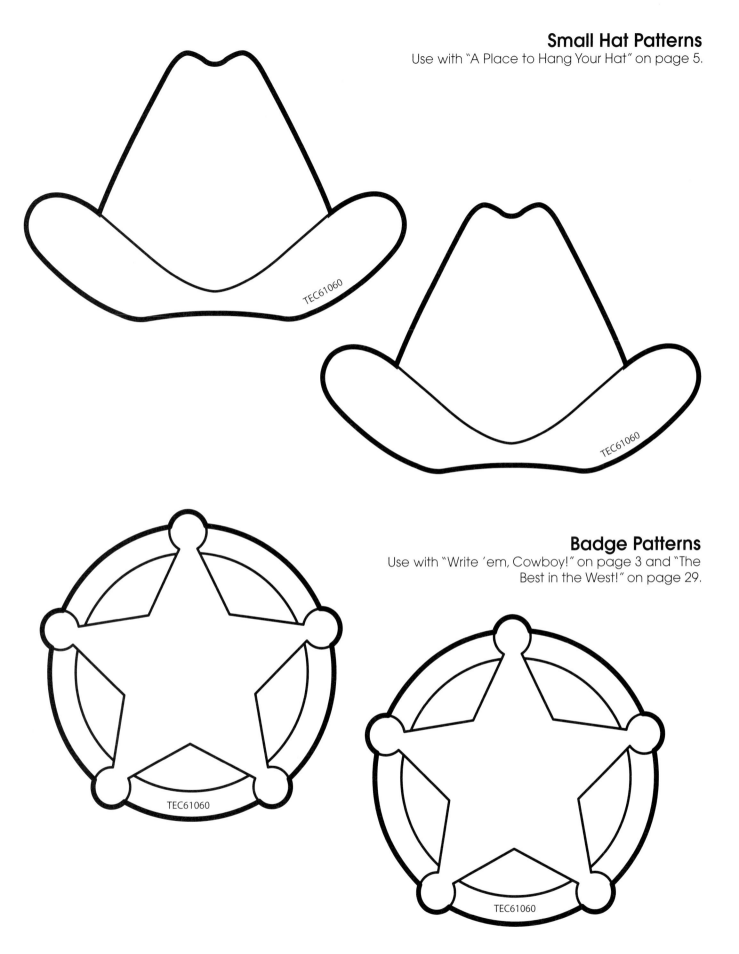

Small Hat Patterns
Use with "A Place to Hang Your Hat" on page 5.

TEC61060

TEC61060

Badge Patterns
Use with "Write 'em, Cowboy!" on page 3 and "The Best in the West!" on page 29.

TEC61060

TEC61060

Cowboy Pattern

Use with "Calling All Cows!" on page 3 and
"A Place to Hang Your Hat" on page 5.

TEC61060

TEC61060

Large Cowboy Hat Pattern
Use with "Hats Off to You!" on page 4.

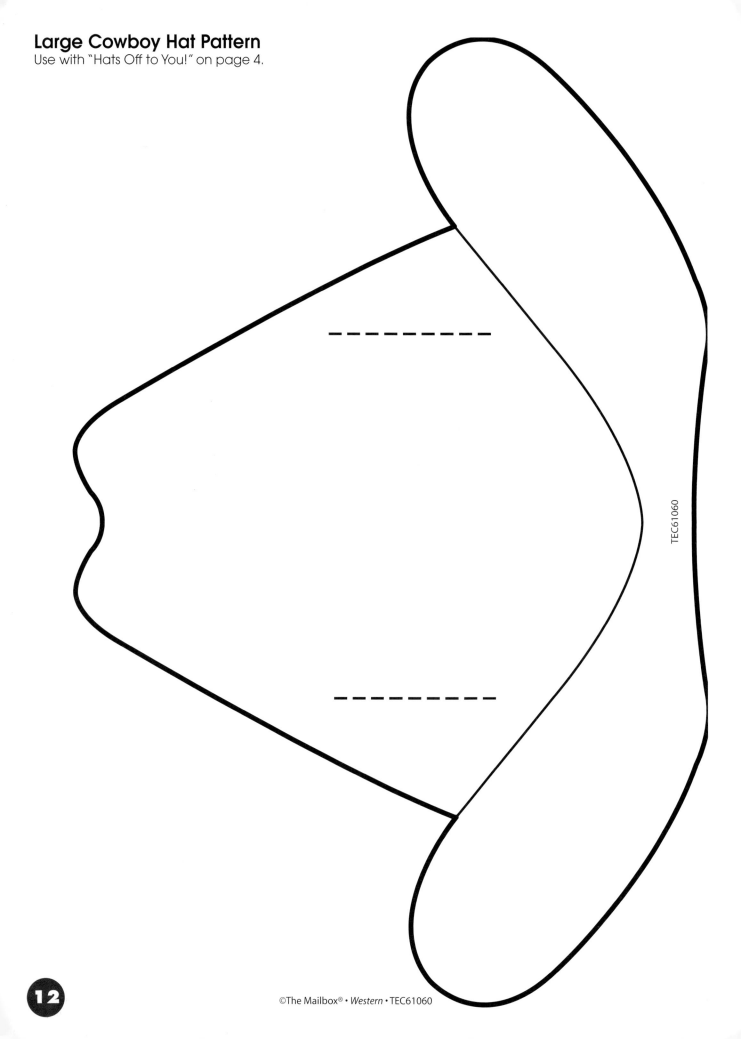

TEC61060

Boot Pattern

Use with "Line Up!" on page 4 and "Give 'em the Boot!" on page 7.

TEC61060

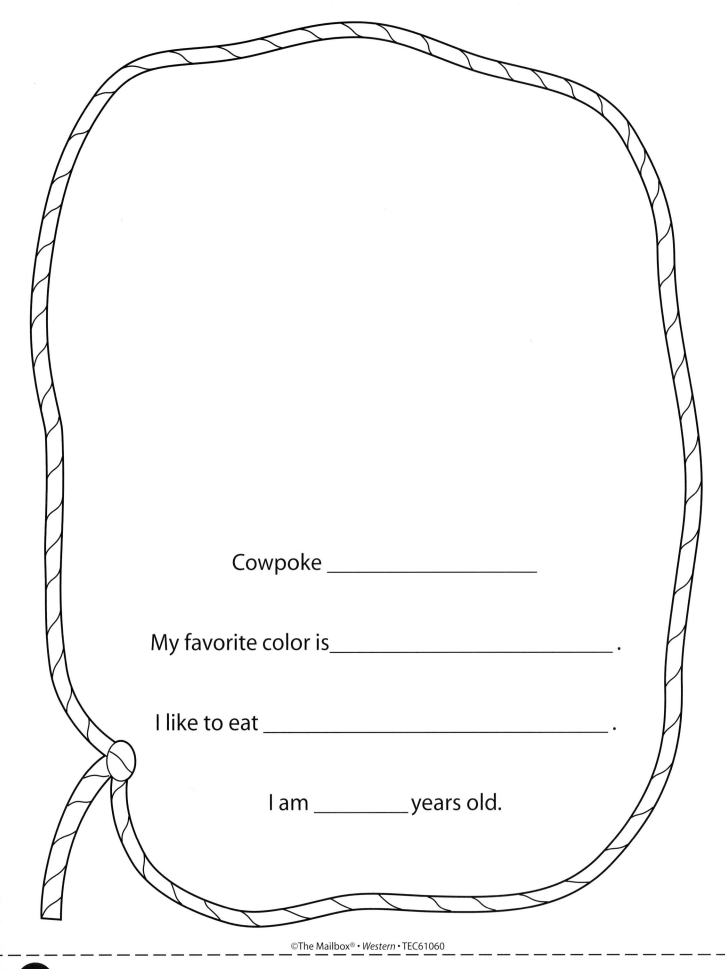

Cowpoke _____

My favorite color is_____ .

I like to eat _____ .

I am _____ years old.

Note to the teacher: Use with "A Rodeo Portfolio" on page 6.

Welcome to the MATH RODEO

Round up your youngsters to develop number comparison skills with the rootin'-tootin' ideas in this unit!

by Rhonda L. Chiles, South Park Elementary, Shawnee Mission, KS

The Rodeo Song

Singing a song

Get your students thinking about the rodeo with a reading of *Armadillo Rodeo* by Jan Brett. Then teach youngsters the rodeo song below. Yippee-yi-yo!

(sung to the tune of "This Old Man")

This cowboy,
He sees one,
One bareback rider having fun.
With a hat on his head
And a yippee-yi-yo!
This cowboy's at the rodeo.

This cowgirl,
She sees two,
Two bronc-riding buckaroos.
With a hat on her head
And a yippee-yi-yo!
This cowgirl's at the rodeo.

This cowboy,
He sees three,
Three calf ropers on bended knee.
With a hat on his head
And a yippee-yi-yo!
This cowboy's at the rodeo.

This cowgirl,
She sees four,
Four steer wrestlers keeping score.
With a hat on her head
And a yippee-yi-yo!
This cowgirl's at the rodeo.

This cowboy,
He sees five,
Five bull riders ready to ride.
With a hat on his head
And a yippee-yi-yo!
This cowboy's at the rodeo.

Rodeo Riders

Comparing two numbers

Have your young cowpokes wear identifying numbers on their backs—just like real rodeo contestants—for this number comparison activity. Program enough sheets of paper each with a different number to make a class set. Tape a number to each student's back and pair students. In turn, have each pair sit on chairs, straddle-style, so that their numbers can be seen by the rest of the class. Instruct students to think about the numbers worn by their classmates and decide which number is larger and which one is smaller. Then ask the group comparison questions such as "Is 13 less than 20?" or "Is 32 greater than or less than 61?" Continue until all students have been riders. Yee-haw!

A Rootin'-Tootin' Card Game

Playing a game
Determining a greater number

This card game will have youngsters looking for larger numbers and then rounding up the herd! To prepare, make two copies of the game cards on page 18. Program each card with a different number from 1 to 20. Color the cards, laminate the pages, and then cut the cards apart. Shuffle the cards and then deal ten cards to each player in a pair. Have each child place her stack of cards facedown in front of her. Then, on the count of three, instruct both players to turn over their top cards. The player with the card that has the greater number keeps both cards. The game continues until one player has all the cards.

> Two is less than eight!

Cowboy Sticks

Counting
Comparing sets of objects

Grab some Unifix cubes for this simple counting and comparing activity. Make two sticks of ten Unifix cubes for each pair of children in your class. Give each child a stick and have him hold it behind his back. Instruct each youngster, in turn, to break his stick and then show it to his partner. Have the partner count the cubes in each stick and then say a number comparison sentence to match the sets using the words *greater than, less than,* or *equal to.* Two is less than eight!

A Cowboy's Favorite Meal—Beans

Identifying greater numbers
Identifying lesser numbers

Serve up this counting activity with a spoon and a bowl of dried beans! To prepare, make a crease down the center of a sheet of paper for each child. Place the creased paper, pencils, a bowl of dried beans, and a tablespoon at a center. Have each child scoop a spoonful of beans next to his paper. Instruct him to count the beans and then write the total on the left side of his paper. Have him repeat the process, but this time instruct him to write the number of beans on the right side of his paper. Have him return the beans to the bowl and circle the greater number and underline the lesser number. If the numbers are equal, have him write an equal sign between the numbers. Then instruct him to repeat the process four more times. It's chow time!

The Barrel Run
Comparing recorded times

A few orange cones (barrels) and two stopwatches are all you need for this time comparison event. Position two sets of three cones outdoors in the formation shown at left, making sure that the cones are at least ten feet apart. Divide students into two teams. Have another adult stand on the opposite side of the finish line and time one team while you time the other team. On your signal, have one child from each team run around each barrel and then across the finish line. Call out each team's time. Instruct the team with the faster (lesser) time to say, "Yee-haw!" After each child has run the race, treat the class to tasty root beer barrel candies!

Crunchy Corrals
Following directions

After all of this number comparison practice, your young buckaroos will be hungry for this snack. Gather the ingredients, utensils, and supplies listed below and then guide each child to make her own crunchy corral snack.

Ingredients for one:
slice of bread
apple jelly
8 pretzel sticks
2 animal crackers

Utensils and supplies:
paper plate for each child
plastic knife for each child

Directions:
1. Spread apple jelly on a slice of bread.
2. Place pretzels around the edges of the bread as shown.
3. Add two animals to your corral.
4. Enjoy!

Game Cards

Use with "A Rootin'-Tootin' Card Game" on page 16.

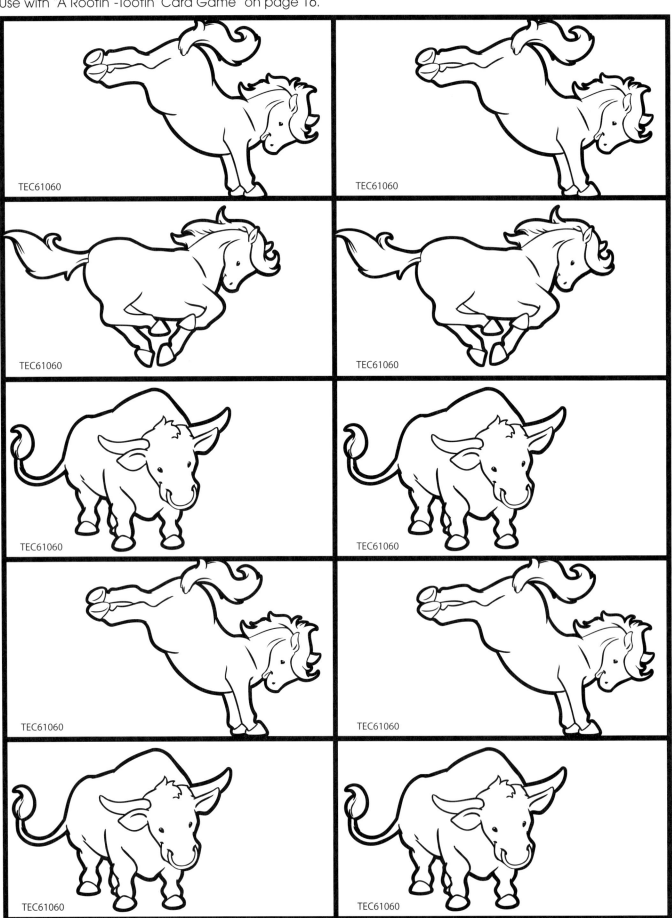

TEC61060

TEC61060

TEC61060

TEC61060

TEC61060

TEC61060

TEC61060

TEC61060

TEC61060

TEC61060

Domino Rodeo

Rustle up excitement for addition and subtraction with these rip-roarin' domino activities!

The ideas corralled in this unit use double-six dominoes. If you'd like to have reproducible dominoes for selected activities, copy the patterns on pages 21 and 22. Your young buckaroos can also use the reproducible dominoes for take-home math practice!

Lassoing Number Combinations
Recognizing different combinations for a number

Lasso a rootin'-tootin' review of number combinations! On a 12" x 18" sheet of construction paper, draw nine rings (lassos) and then number them 2 through 10. Laminate the resulting workmat for durability. Remove from a set of dominoes the tiles with the following numbers of dots: 0, 1, 11, 12. Place the remaining dominoes, the workmat, and a supply of paper at a center. Have students visit the center in pairs.

In turn, each student takes one domino, names the number combination represented by the dots, and then places the domino in the lasso with the corresponding sum. Students continue taking turns until all of the dominoes are sorted. Then each youngster removes the dominoes from a chosen lasso and writes an addition sentence for each domino. Yee-haw!

adapted from an idea by Colleen Fitzgerald
Sylvania, OH

Uh-oh, Domino!
Adding with visual aids

You can sum up this partner game with one word—*fun!* To prepare, two students remove from a set of dominoes one tile for each of these sums: 0, 1, 4, 5, 7, 8, 11, 12. (Provide assistance as needed.) The youngsters use the remaining dominoes and the directions below to play a modified version of Go Fish. Addition success is guaranteed!

Directions:
1. The players sit facing each other and arrange the dominoes facedown between them.
2. Each player takes four dominoes and stands them so the dots face her. She sets aside any pairs of dominoes with identical sums.
3. Player 1 asks Player 2, "Do you have a domino that shows a sum of [number]?"
4. If Player 2 does, she states the addition fact and hands the domino to Player 1, who sets the domino pair aside. If Player 2 does not have a requested domino, she says, "Uh-oh, domino!" and Player 1 takes another domino, if possible.
5. Player 2 takes a turn in the same manner.
6. Alternate play continues, with players setting aside any domino pairs, until one player has no dominoes left to play or the stock runs out. The player with more domino pairs wins.

Heather Graley, Columbus, OH

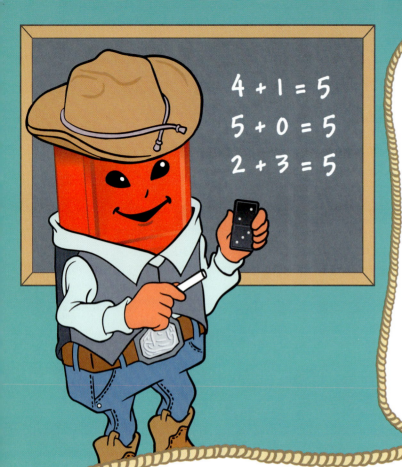

$$4 + 1 = 5$$
$$5 + 0 = 5$$
$$2 + 3 = 5$$

Number Sentence Stampede
Writing number sentences

Round up addition sentences with a skill-boosting version of musical chairs! Assign one student to be the announcer. Have him put his chair aside and stand by the board. Give one domino to each seated student. To play one round, the announcer rolls two dice and states the sum. Each student who has a domino with this total takes it to the board, and the announcer takes a seat in an empty chair. (If no students have a corresponding domino, the announcer rolls again.) Each student at the board quickly writes an addition sentence for his domino and then looks for an empty chair to sit in. The student who does not get a chair leads the students in reading the number sentences and becomes the next announcer.

To begin another round, the new announcer hands his domino to the previous announcer, erases the board, and signals students to trade dominoes. The activity continues as time allows. To play a subtraction version, the announcer rolls one die and students check for dominoes that have this difference.

Heather Graley, Columbus, OH

Wanted: Largest Sum!
Identifying and comparing sums

Young wranglers compare sums with this domino showdown! Prepare for small-group play by giving every two or three students a paper lunch bag that contains a set of dominoes. To play one round, each player, in turn, takes one domino from the bag. She sets it down and states a corresponding addition fact. The player with the largest sum takes all the dominoes played in that round. If two or more players have the same sum, they each take one more domino to compare. Additional rounds are played until there are fewer dominoes in the bag than players. The player with the most dominoes wins.

Game variation: If two or more students have the same sum, each youngster subtracts the dots on her domino. The player with the smallest difference wins the round!

Kimberly Bowsher, Crabapple Crossing Elementary, Alpharetta, GA

Colleen Fitzgerald, Sylvania, OH

Fact-Family Chow
Identifying fact families

Tempting domino look-alikes make fact-family practice a treat! Each student needs a paper plate, one graham cracker, a two-inch length of licorice rope, and 12 white or brown chocolate chips. Ask each student to use his licorice to divide his graham cracker in half as shown. Then have him arrange his chocolate chips on his cracker to resemble a designated domino number combination. Ask volunteers to name the corresponding addition and subtraction facts; write them on the board. Instruct students to clear their crackers. Announce a different number combination to continue. After a desired amount of practice, invite students to eat their treats. Mmm!

Laurie Shaw, Southeast Primary School, Ravenna, OH

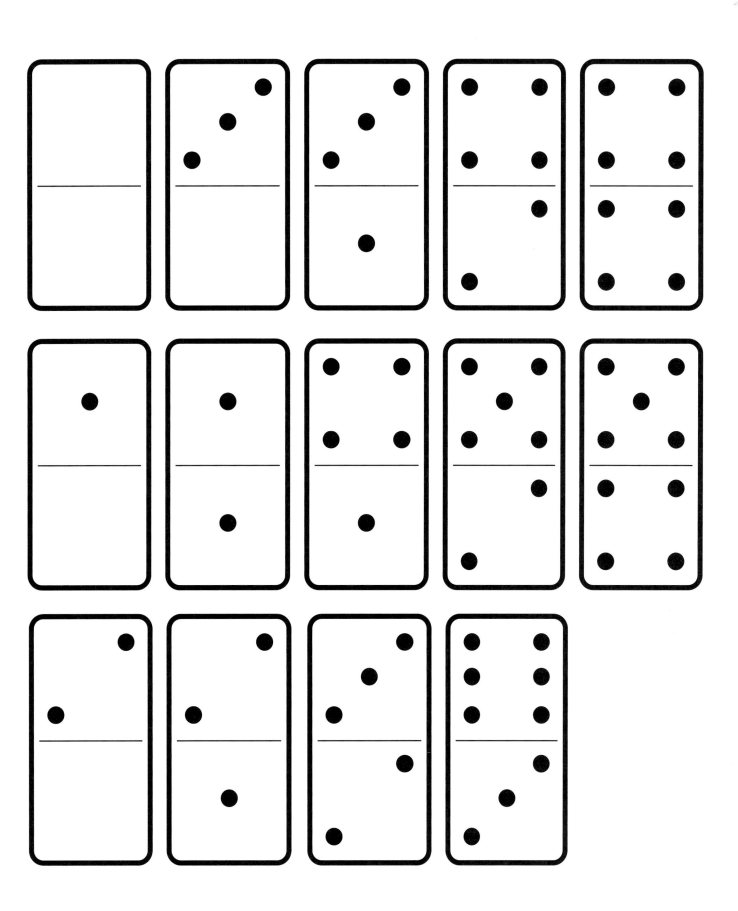

Note to the teacher: Use with the ideas on pages 19 and 20.

21

Note to the teacher: Use with the ideas on pages 19 and 20.

SENTENCE STAMPEDE

Howdy, pardner! Saddle up your buckaroos for this boot-scootin' review of sentences!

ideas by Vicki Dabrowka

GROCERIES

SENTENCE SHOWDOWN
Complete and incomplete sentences

Corral your cowpokes for a sentence showdown! To prepare, program individual sentence strips with complete and incomplete sentences. Also have each student label a yellow tagboard star cutout "Deputy [student's name]." Gather students, making sure each deputy has her personalized badge. Display a prepared sentence strip, read it aloud, and pause. Then say "Deputies, cast your votes!" If a child believes the sentence is complete, she does nothing. If she believes the sentence is incomplete, she holds her badge high above her head. Follow up each vote by asking a volunteer to explain why the sentence is complete (incomplete). If a sentence is incomplete, have volunteers complete it in different ways. Continue the showdown in this manner until every sentence strip is judged or time runs out. To keep your cowpokes' skills sharp, schedule additional sentence showdowns!

FOUR-PART RODEO
Sentence types

Yee-haw! Wranglers team up to show off their sentence skills at this rip-roarin' rodeo. After a review of the four sentence types (statements, commands, questions, exclamations), divide students into four groups. Name each group for a different sentence type and teach each group a rodeo response. (See "Rodeo Responses" below.) To start the rodeo, announce a sentence. Allow time for each group to determine the sentence type. Then, on your signal, the group named for the type of sentence shared gives its rodeo response. Continue in this manner, making sure that each group receives equal opportunities to respond. For a post-rodeo challenge, write several sentences on the board, omitting ending punctuation. Ask each child to copy and punctuate the sentences and then label each one with its sentence type.

Deputy Darlene

Rodeo Responses

Group	Response
Statements	We are wranglers.
Questions	What's up?
Commands	Stop right there, pardner.
Exclamations	Yee-haw!

More Rootin'-

Pioneer Life From A to Z

By Bobbie Kalman
Published by Crabtree Publishing Company

A *is for apples,* B *is for bee,* C *is for churn…and so on, you see! There's something for every letter of the alphabet in this informative book about pioneer life. Photographs, illustrations, and historical paintings teach readers about objects, events, and places familiar to the pioneers.*

Since you'll probably prefer to share this book in segments rather than all at once, try this idea. Place a set of magnetic letters in a basket. During a group time, personalize the following chant with a specific student's name and have that child pick a letter from the basket and place it on a magnetic board. Then read the corresponding page or pages from the book. Afterward, write the pioneer word of the day next to the magnetic letter on your board.

V village
B bee
R rag rugs
J journal

Let's learn about the pioneers.
Let's read from *A to Z.*
Pull a letter, [child's name].
What letter will it be?

A Little Prairie House

From the My First Little House Books series
By Laura Ingalls Wilder
Illustrated by Renée Graef

The Ingalls family has left the Big Woods of Wisconsin and is traveling west to build a new home on the prairie. The prairie is lonesome and scary at first, but soon a neighbor comes to help Pa and their new house is almost finished!

After seeing Laura's excitement about her new house, your youngsters will be happy to build log houses of their own—edible ones! To prepare, tint white frosting with green food coloring. Give each child in a small group a paper plate, a plastic knife, a square graham cracker (two sections), and a handful of pretzel sticks. Set a container of cream cheese and the container of green frosting on the table.

Have each child spread some frosting across his plate to resemble prairie grass. Then have him spread cream cheese on his graham cracker and set it on the grass. Next, have him arrange pretzel sticks in the cream cheese to resemble the logs and sloped roof of his cabin. (Have him break the pretzel sticks into shorter pieces as needed.) After admiring these palatable prairie houses, invite your youngsters to eat 'em up!

Tootin' Ideas

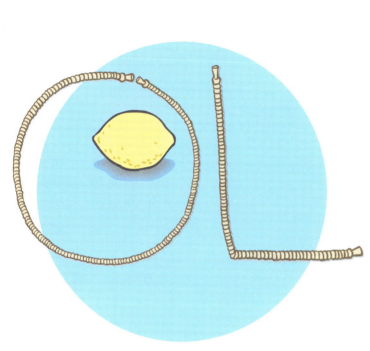

L Is for Letter Lasso

This simple activity will have students practicing letter formation and searching for things that begin with the **letter *l***. Cut 18-inch lengths of rope so that each child will have one piece. Knot the ends of each piece to prevent fraying. Gather several items that begin with the letter *l* and a few that do not begin with *l*. Seat students on the floor in a circle and place the items in the center. In turn, give each child a rope and have her lasso (lay her rope in a circle) an item that begins with the /l/ sound. Have youngsters practice the /l/ sound each time a child encircles an item with her rope. After each child has had a turn, collect the items and then instruct each student to use her rope to practice forming upper-case and lowercase *l*'s on the floor.

Sherri Martin
Southland Academy
Montezuma, GA

Rodeo Roundup

Yee-haw! Encourage your young cowpokes to **count** and corral some horses with this easy math game! To prepare, duplicate page 30 to make a class supply. Have each child color and cut out the horses at the bottom of her sheet. Then have students play the game in pairs. One child at a time rolls a die and identifies the number rolled. Then she covers the corresponding number on her reproducible with one of her horses, ending her turn. If she rolls a number she has already covered, her turn ends. The first child to cover all her numbers—and have all her horses in the corral—is the winner!

Rhonda L. Chiles
South Park Elementary School
Shawnee Mission, KS

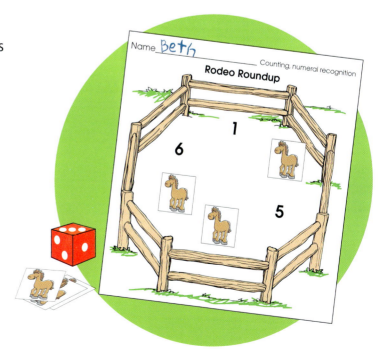

25

Yee-Haw!

Enhance a Wild West theme with this **following directions** game. Designate one child to be It. Divide the remainder of the group into threes. Have two children in each threesome hold hands to form a corral. Have the third child stand inside the corral and play the part of a little dogie, or calf, that's been rounded up! When the animals are in the corrals, have It give a starting signal by shouting, "Yee-haw!" Each little dogie then ducks out of her corral and runs to a new one. At the same time, It tries to run into one of the corrals. The little dogie left without a corral becomes It for the next round. Now that's some mighty fine fun!

Susan Bunyan
Linn Elementary
Dodge City, KS

A Rootin'-Tootin' Roundup

All you need for this **skill review center** is a stash of extra skill sheets from the past school year. Store several pages in a cowboy hat. Place the hat, a container of pencils, and a few bandanas at a center. A student completes as many skill sheets as time allows. Restock the hat as needed. Now that's a center that's long on usefulness and short on preparation time! Yee-haw!

Renee Carnochan
Solley Elementary
Glen Burnie, MD

Hobbyhorse

Round up these horses that offer artistic opportunities and lots of **fine-motor practice** with a purpose. To begin, draw the head of a horse onto tagboard; then cut it out. Punch holes along the pattern where the mane will be. Color the horse as desired. Fold a length of yarn in half. Thread the folded end of the yarn through one of the holes; then poke the two loose ends through that yarn loop. Pull on the loose ends until the yarn is secure against the horse. Repeat this process to create a mane along the horse's neck and forehead. If desired, make stick puppets by hot-gluing wooden paint stirrers to the backs of the horses. Or even make "riding" horses by hot gluing wooden yardsticks or dowels to the backs. Encourage children to use their horses in dramatic play. Giddy up!

Pat Gaddis
St. Stephen's Methodist Church
Houston, TX

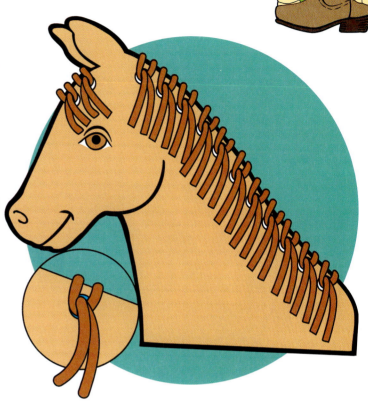

Wagons Ho!

Transform a rectangular classroom table into a covered wagon to make an **imaginative play area**! Set the table upside down on the floor. Use heavy-duty tape to attach large pieces of cardboard (as shown), bending the cardboard into a rounded shape as you go. Help little ones paint the cardboard to resemble the top of a covered wagon. Then attach four giant cardboard circles to the sides and paint them to look like wagon wheels. Ready? Go west!

Trish Draper
Millarville Community School
Millarville, Alberta, Canada

Cutie-Pie Cowpoke

Saddle up for this rootin'-tootin' art project! You just may lasso some of your buckaroos' geometry skills, too!

Materials for one cowpoke:

two 6" squares of light blue construction paper (pants)
one 6" square of dark blue construction paper (shirt)
one 3" square of red construction paper (bandana)
one 3" circle of skin-toned construction paper (head)
one brown construction paper copy of the hat, boot,
   and glove patterns on page 31

construction paper scraps
markers or crayons
scissors
glue

Steps:

1. Cut out the hat, boot, and glove patterns. Set them aside.
2. To make the body, fold each of the three 6-inch squares in half to create a triangle. Position the dark blue triangle (shirt) with the fold at the top. Unfold the paper and glue each glove cutout directly below the crease line. Next, glue the two light blue triangles in place to create pants; then refold the shirt and glue it closed.
3. Glue each boot cutout to the bottom of a pant leg.
4. To make the bandana, fold the red construction paper square in half to create a triangle; then slide the top of the shirt inside the resulting bandana and glue the bandana in place.
5. Glue the hat cutout to the top of the skin-toned circle. Use markers or crayons to add facial features to the circle; then glue the resulting head to the top of the bandana.
6. Use the construction paper scraps and markers to decorate your cowpoke.

Kim Clemente, Schnieder Grade School, Farmer City, IL

What a Horse!

Make a class supply of the horse pattern on page 32 onto construction paper. Provide each child with a copy and have him cut out the horse shape on the heavy dark outlines. Have each child color his cutout, then fold the horse on the dotted line. Have each student glue a few lengths of yarn on the horse to resemble a tail. Then have him clip two clothespins to the horse to resemble the horse's legs.

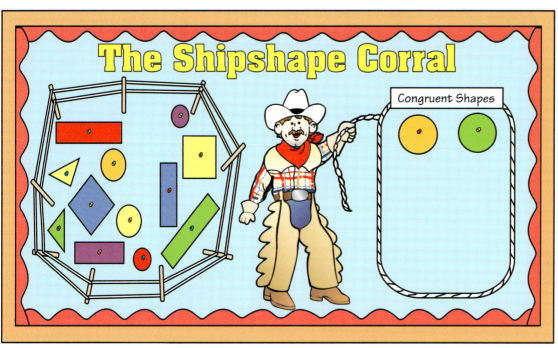

Showcase a corral, a cowpoke (if desired enlarge the cowboy pattern on page 10), and the title. To reinforce congruence, label the lasso as shown. Using pushpins, randomly display pairs of **congruent shapes** inside the corral. Every few days select volunteers to round up congruent pairs from the corral and display them inside the lasso. To reinforce symmetry, retitle the lasso and stock the corral with a collection of cutouts that includes several symmetrical shapes.

Lasso your wranglers' **outstanding work** at this star-studded display. Post a cowboy (if desired enlarge the cowboy pattern on page 10) and title. Have each youngster create a personalized badge from the pattern on page 9 and then round up a sample of his finest work. Display each work sample with its corresponding badge. To keep the display current, invite wranglers to replace their work as frequently as desired.

Kathy Marquar, J. E. Moss Elementary, Antioch, TN

Rodeo Roundup

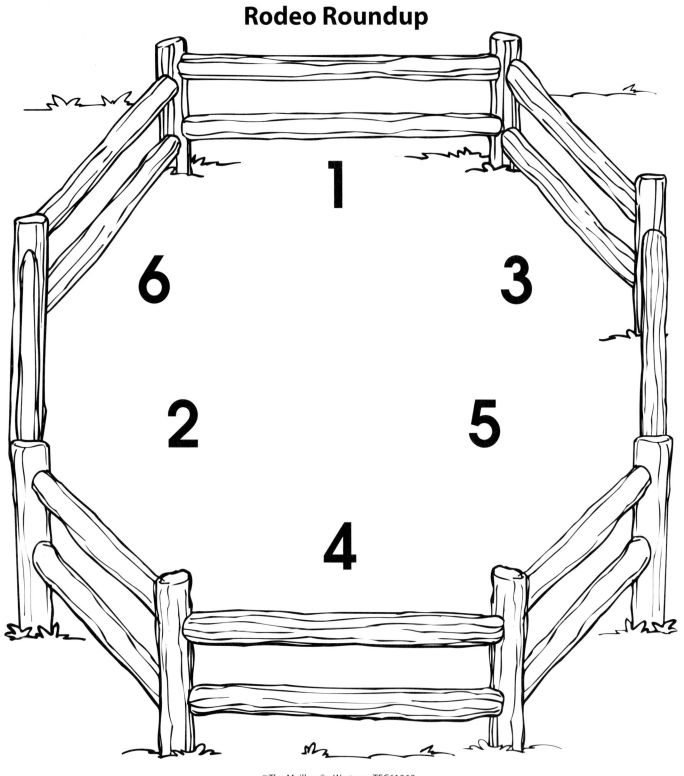

1

6   3

2   5

4

30 **Note to the teacher:** Use with "Rodeo Roundup" on page 25.

Cowboy Patterns
Use the hat, boot, and glove patterns
with "Cutie-Pie Cowpoke" on page 28.

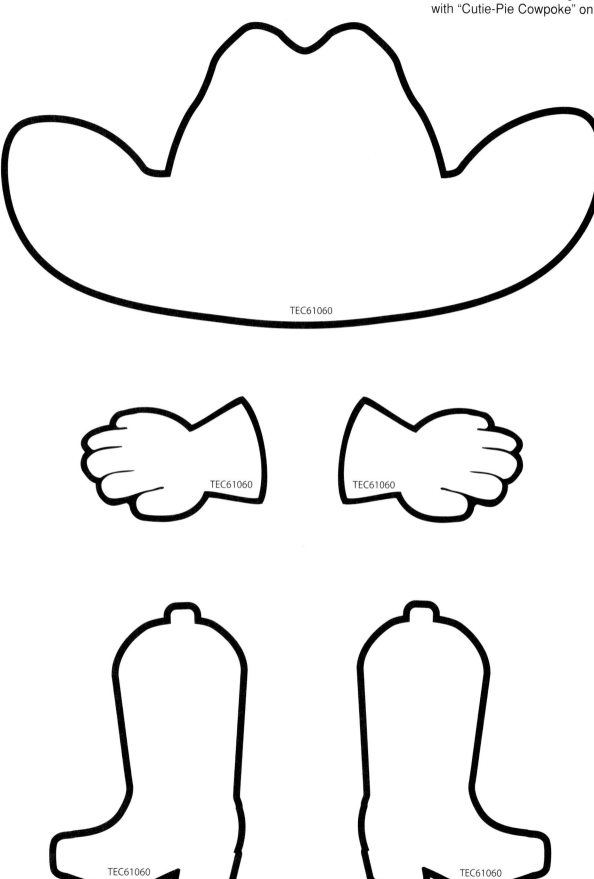

TEC61060

TEC61060

TEC61060

TEC61060

TEC61060

Horse Pattern

Use with "What a Horse!" on page 28.

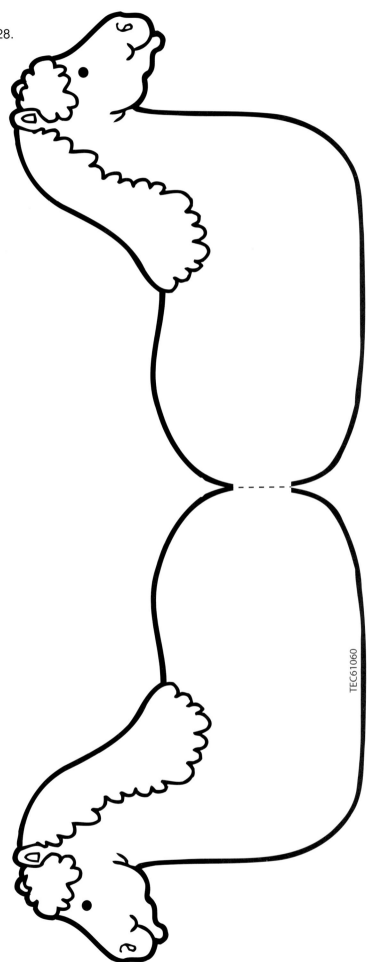

TEC61060

Name _____

Come and Get It!

✂ Cut.

Put the pictures in order.

Glue.

④ What comes next? Draw on the back of your paper.

Name _____

Chuck-Wagon Chow

 Cut.

Put the pictures in order.

Glue.

What comes next? Draw on the back of your paper.

34

Name _____

Chuck-Wagon ABCs

A	B	C	D		F
H		J		L	M
N			Q	R	
		V		X	

✏ Write.

Read.

Bales and Buddies

Color the pictures that match the beginning sound.

Name _____

A Pony Picnic

Circle the letter that shows the beginning sound.

r · s

s · r

t · v

t · w

v · s

r · t

v · w

Name _____

Corral Counting

✋ Count.

✏️ Write the number.

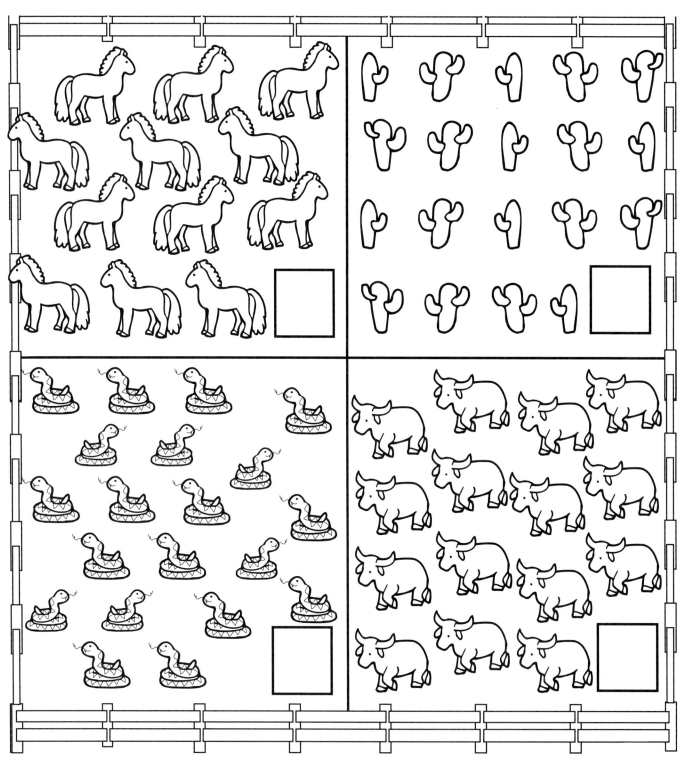

Bonus Box: On the back of this paper, draw 16 cowboy hats.

©The Mailbox® • *Western* • TEC61060

Horse Counters

If desired, have each child use a copy of the horse counters with pages 40 and 41.

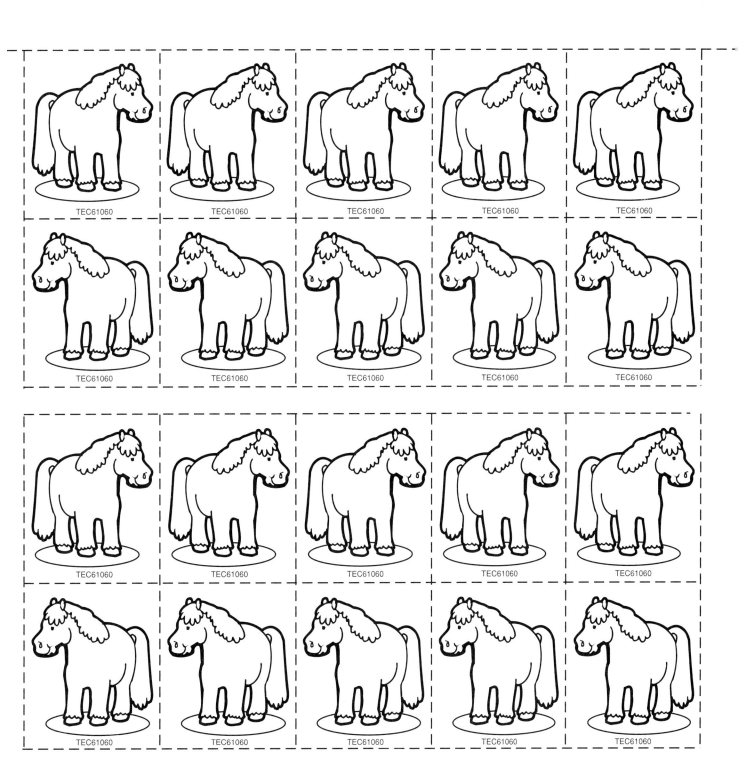

TEC61060
TEC61060
TEC61060
TEC61060
TEC61060
TEC61060
TEC61060
TEC61060
TEC61060
TEC61060
TEC61060
TEC61060
TEC61060
TEC61060
TEC61060
TEC61060
TEC61060
TEC61060
TEC61060
TEC61060

Buckaroo Mouse

Add.

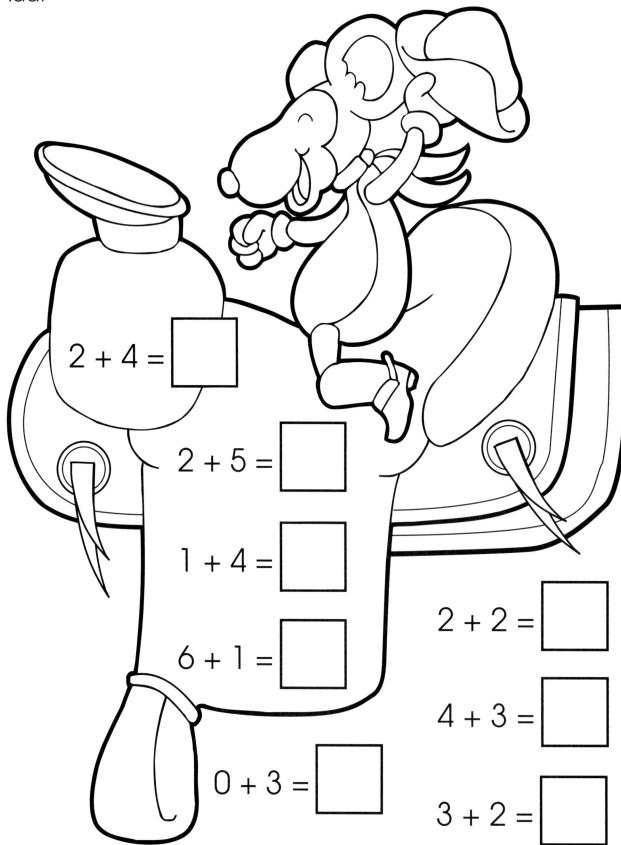

$2 + 4 =$ ☐

$2 + 5 =$ ☐

$1 + 4 =$ ☐

$6 + 1 =$ ☐

$2 + 2 =$ ☐

$4 + 3 =$ ☐

$0 + 3 =$ ☐

$3 + 2 =$ ☐

Name _____

Rootin'-Tootin' Boots

Add.

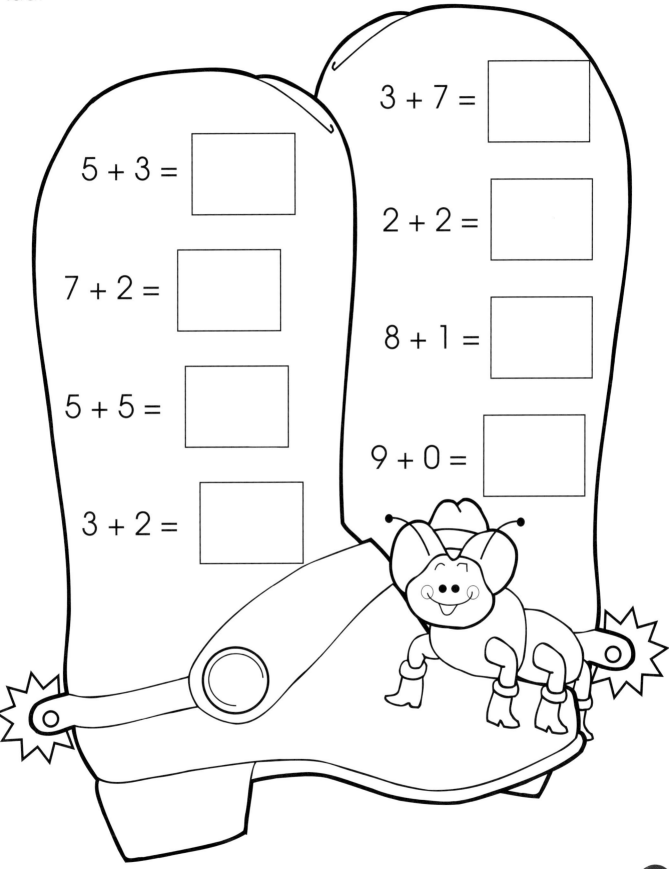

5 + 3 =

7 + 2 =

5 + 5 =

3 + 2 =

3 + 7 =

2 + 2 =

8 + 1 =

9 + 0 =

Rulers

Have each child use a ruler cutout to complete pages 43 and 44.

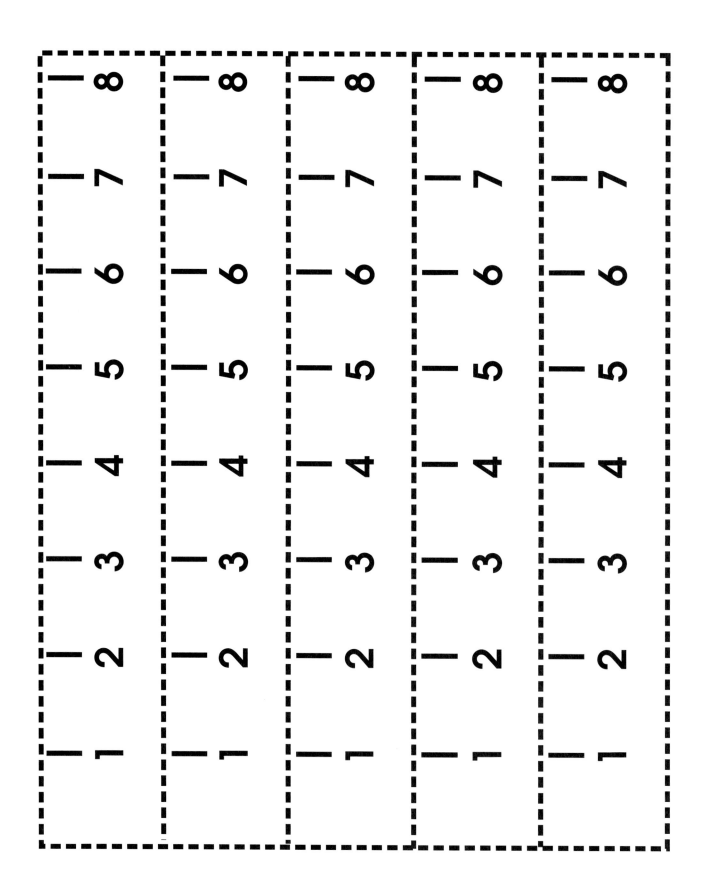

Fence by the Inch

Measure each fence.

 Cut. Glue the number of inches.

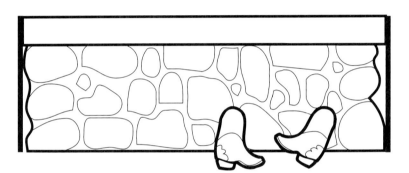

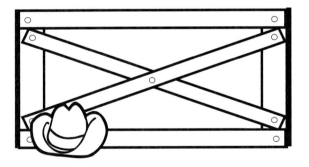

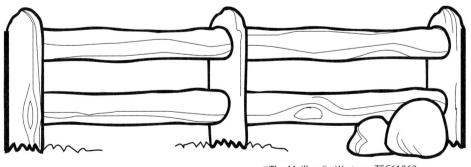

| 2 | 5 | 6 | 4 | 8 | 3 |

43

Cactus Cuties

Measure.

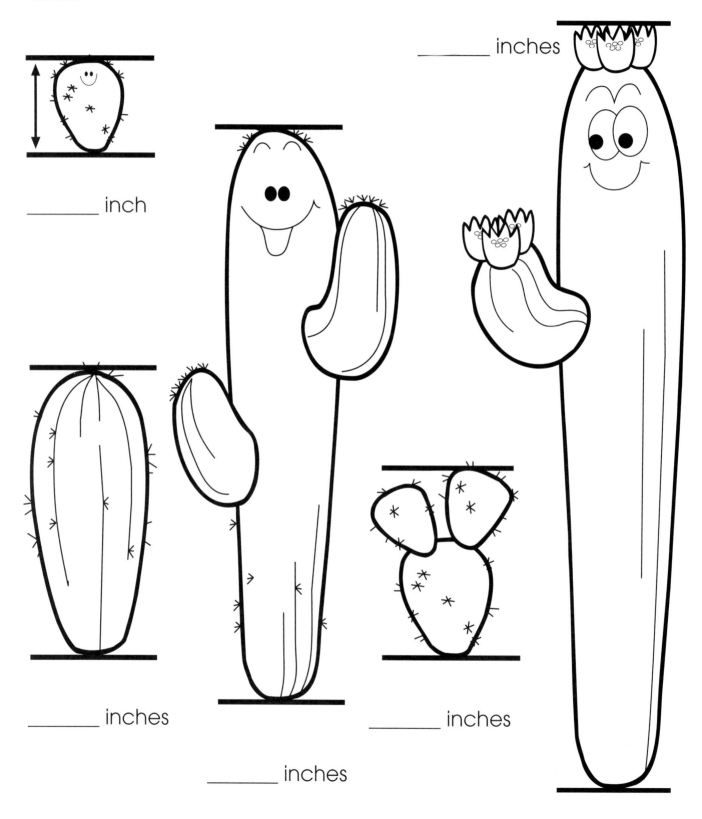 Write the numeral.

_____ inches

_____ inch

_____ inches

_____ inches

_____ inches

_____ inches

Roundup Time

 Cut.

Glue to show the time.

12:00	4:00	10:00
8:00	1:00	6:00

High Noon

Write each time.

_____:_____   _____:_____   _____:_____   _____:_____

_____:_____   _____:_____

_____:_____

Programmable Activity Cards

Duplicate this page several times on construction paper. Color the cowboy boots, laminate them, and then cut them out. Use a permanent marker to program the boots with matching skills of your choice. (For example, program half of the boots with addition problems and the other half with the corresponding sums.) To do this activity, a child matches each boot to a corresponding card.

Finished Sample

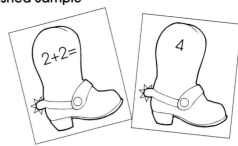

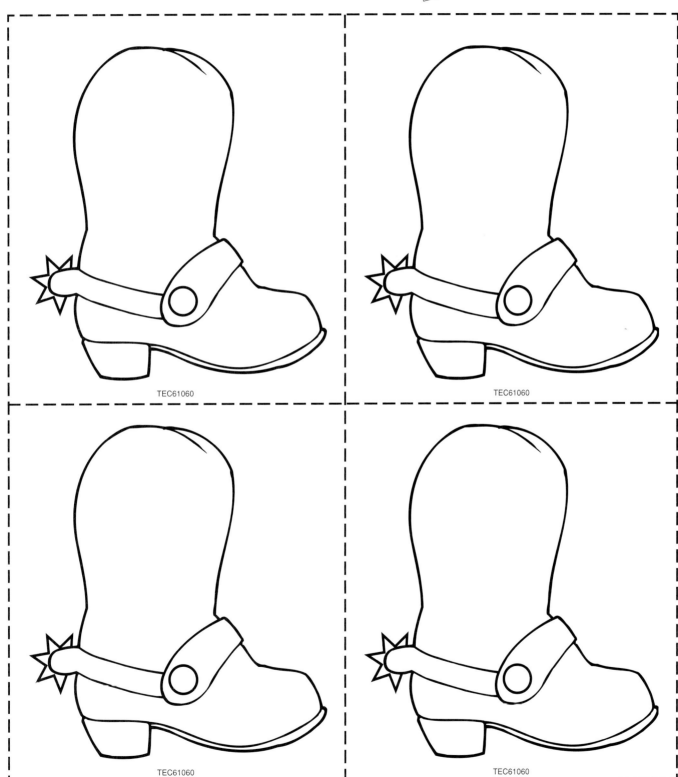

TEC61060

TEC61060

TEC61060

TEC61060

_____

Note to the teacher: Copy and personalize an award for each child.